Bloom

Carly Rowe

BookLeaf Publishing

Presentation by *BookLeaf Publishing*

Web: www.bookleafpub.com

E-mail: info@bookleafpub.com

ISBN: 9789357441308

First edition 2023

ACKNOWLEDGEMENT

Thank you to all my friends who never made me feel crazy.

The Blues

Suddenly,
I realized that this is all my life would be
Stuck in this place, dreams remaining out of reach
And I cried for days.

Foolishly
I held onto this notion that I was special
In spite of all the evidence that I was not
And I cried for days.

Dismally
I lost all hope that I could change
But I am just an ordinary nobody
And I cried for days.

Ghosts

My sister is dead
And truth be told, I don't think of her often.
I couldn't save her.
But worse, did I try?
I watched her unravel
Helpless, out of my league.

But sometimes I feel her presence
Even when my brain works overtime to keep her out
And she lets me know I did all right
That no one could save her
But even as her ghost comforts me
Embracing me in dreams
I still feel haunted.

Nothing

You gave me nothing
and I relished in it.
I took the emptiness
filled it with my own fantasies
where you entertain a woman like me
allow me to shower you in ffection
I submit. I beg. I give.
Even in my wildest dreams I'm not worth loving
So I take your nothing
and I relish in it.

Who's Controlling Who?

Shape shifter.
Witch.
A few subtle shifts and I am exactly who you need me to be.
Puppet. Marionette.
Play my strings right and I am exactly who you want me to be.

Senseless Running

Going nowhere, but I'm running fast
Like a treadmill locked in a windowless room.
What would happen if I stopped running?
Would I notice the walls? See a door?
But which fate is worse
Going nowhere in a familiar place or
going anywhere?

me and the moon.

I'm mad at you today, I scream at the moon
I shake my fist and look to the heavens
What else can I do to appease the glorious globe
in the sky?
I work through her moods
Embrace the shadow and dance in her beams
and I beg of her to change the tides.

relief.

I am not who I thought I was.
A warrior, a soldier.
Forged from steel.
Unlovable cold.

I am not who I thought I was
and for that, I am relieved.

Shrug.

I ask him, are you happy?
He says that he is fine.
And yet, his eyes drift toward the floor
Avert my gaze as his lips so slightly turn down
I study his face and think to myself
I can't remember the last time I've heard him laugh.
I think, maybe, at my house?
On my couch after a few glasses of wine
But before that? I can't be too sure.
Many of our memories are rimmed with tears
I ask him again, are you happy?
He shrugs.

Let's not try

I cannot fix the man who does not want to be fixed.
I know this. You know this.
But on one hand, I could try
until eventually your patience with me wears thin
my love becomes suffocating, a hand around your neck
Maddening us both until we become creatures we no longer recognize.
Never mind. Let's just call it now
while we remain in our human forms, and you still think of me fondly.

Mysterious

Who will I be when I'm happy?
What will that feel like?
An unruly existence is all I have known
Truthfully, I've come to enjoy the chaos
I cling to the anger, too afraid to let go
Because who knows who I will be when I finally know peace.

Journey

I took a trip to my subconscious once.
I traveled down a dark hole, across a river of ether
and to a forest in the depths of my spirit.
I wanted to find what was calling so loudly
What unknown force beckoned me to depth
uncharted.

I found myself in front of a tree
Dead. Rotting. Black.
I wept and hung my head, unable to face my shame
and a past I locked away where no one could ever
find.
Why? was all I could muster to the mass of rotten
wood
No response and I began to lose hope.

But still, I heard the call.
I lifted my eyes to the rotted tree, and knew
there were no answers here, just misery, guilt and
shame.
I walked away from this place, following my
unknown guide
to a willow tree.
Majest. Strong. Gold.

I wept and lifted my eyes to a light that felt familiar.
Why is all I could whisper.
I received no answer, but I could comprehend that the question I asked was wrong.
And I knew that all this time I had been
forgive me
climbing the wrong tree.

Bloom

I can't go home; the answer isn't there.
It's not even home any longer
Just a city that's moved on and forgotten me.
I could scour the streets I used to know
A never-ending search for the girl I used to be.
Instead, I settle for where I am planted.
The conditions are hard and most days I struggle
to find the sun
But grow, I must.
And so, I bloom.

Crush

Who is he? Where did he come from?
How did he get here, in my bed?
I feel that pull of excitement again
I didn't think I could after the way my last love broke me
leaving me in pieces that are now barely held together
But he moves slowly, thoughtfully
Tip toes through my head quietly, softly, easily
like he's been here before.
I'm savoring the sweetness of this crush
Afraid to overindulge too soon
before it crushes me.

Neruda

At the breakfast table I drink coffee
My daughter eats an egg and
Shares blueberries with the dog.
On Friday we do love spells
I read her Pablo Neruda in fractured Spanish
The love I conjure already here
I rarely sit still enough to see it.

Modern poet

How lucky are we?
To be poets in the age of technology.
I can write my prose with my thumbs
in the bathtub floating to transcendence
Allowing art to flow through my fingertips
Thoughts knowing no limits
Untethered to the pen and paper
Available to the masses
And all it takes is my mind and a click
My self is shared.

Small act of bravery

I wrote this poem specifically to share
A promise made to myself
That I'd share this with someone, anyone
outside of my own skin.
I'm terrified because the ego tells me that
People may only exist if they look a certain way
Live a certain way
Remain unscarred by life.
It's debilitating to believe your existence is too
shameful to share
I don't know who will read this
And if it is taken in good humor or disgust
But it's a piece of me out there now
Daring to be connect

Bittersweet

I'm not asking for too much.
I'll take violence if it's intertwined with love
Give me extra bitter, but don't forget the sweet.

I notice random acts of kindness between
strangers
and it moves me to tears.
Because if I can witness small acts of love
Surely, it can happen to me?

puzzle

All I ask of my next lover
is that if they choose to see me
as a jigsaw puzzle that needs to be solved
at least be patient.

www.ingramcontent.com/pod-product-compliance
Lightning Source LLC
Chambersburg PA
CBHW051722130826
49812CB00034B/1304
* 9 7 8 9 3 5 7 4 4 1 3 0 8 *